Just Sushi

A Collection of Simple Sushi Recipes

BY

PJ Group Publishing

Copyright © - All Rights Reserved

This Book is licensed for your personal enjoyment only. It may not be copied or reproduced in any format including print or digital unless permission is obtained the copyright holder.

The content of this book has been reviewed for accuracy. However, the author and publisher disclaim any liability for any damages, losses, or injuries that my result from the use or misuse of any product or information presented herein. It is the purchaser's responsibility to read and follow all instructions and warnings on all product labels.

ISBN-13:978-1489578822

ISBN-10:148957882X

CONTENTS

Introduction... 5

The Basics... 6

    Sushi Rice 7

    Tossa Shoyu... 9

    Ponzu.. 11

    Gari 13

Nigiri... 15

    Salmon Nigiri... 16

    Tuna Nigiri... 18

    Ebi Nigiri 20

    Tamago Nigiri.. 22

Norimaki 25

    Shichimi Norimaki................................. 26

    Salmon and Asparagus Norimaki 28

    Shrimp and Avocado Norimaki 31

    Crab Asparagus and Shiitake Norimaki with Ponzu Sauce.. 33

    Dragon Roll.. 35

    California Roll 38

    Inside-out California Norimaki.............. 40

    Inside out Salmon Norimaki.................. 42

Gunkan.. 44

    Tobiko Gunkanzushi.............................. 45

    Salmon Roe Gunkanzushi...................... 47

    Negitoro Gunkanzushi 49

Crayfish and Mango Gunkanzushi 51

Lemon Pepper Crab Gunkanzushi 53

Greenbeans Gunkanzushi with Gomadare Sauce 55

Temaki 57

Unagi Temaki 58

Tuna Temaki 60

Squid Temaki 62

Salmon Temaki with Sweet Chili Sauce 64

Crispy Salmon Skin Temaki 66

Codfish Temaki with Tartar Sauce 68

Vegetarian Temaki 70

Chirashizushi 72

Tokyo-style Chirashizushi 73

Shrimp and Crab Chirashizushi 75

Lobster Chirashizushi with Wasabi Mayonnaise 76

Smoked Mackerel Chirashizushi 77

Oshizushi 78

Smoked Salmon with Avocado Oshizushi 79

Teriyaki Tuna Oshizushi 81

Scallop Oshizushi 83

Introduction

Sushi is definitely one of the most popular Japanese foods – both inside and outside of the country. These delicious nuggets of flavor are loved not only for their fresh, clean taste but how they look as well. A well-made platter of sushi can often resemble a work of art in itself! And perhaps, this is one of the reasons why sushi is often eaten as part of a celebratory meal. It is both a feast for the stomach and the eyes as well.

While sushi might be daunting to re-create at home, all you'd really need is practice, practice and more practice! This book will help you on your sushi-making journey - the 35 specially selected recipes are all relatively easy. Just Sushi: A Collection of Simple Sushi Recipes will how to make yummy and beautiful sushi, the easy way!

The Basics

In making sushi, there are some materials that you would need. First is a bamboo rolling mat. This is used for making rolled sushi types such as maki. Or if you prefer the easy way, there are actually sushi-making kits available on the market today that doesn't involve the use of the traditional rolling mat.

Second, you will need a sushi-oke. It's a large, shallow, wooden bowl specifically used for making sushi rice. Since it's made of wood, it doesn't conduct heat, allowing the rice to cool down substantially.

Sushi Rice

The first thing that you need to learn in making sushi is to know how to make good sushi rice or shari. Shari is the foundation of every good sushi - without it, you won't be able to make a delicious sushi. Use only japonica rice or sushi rice variety.

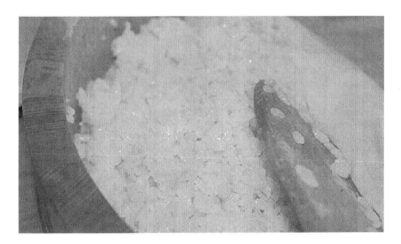

Makes 2 cups cooked rice.

Ingredients:

- 9 oz. japonica or sushi rice
- 1 ½ cups water
- 1 pc. konbu or kelp (Available in most Asian groceries.)
- 2 tbsp. awase-zu or sushi vinegar mix (Available in most Asian groceries.)

Method:

1.Wash the rice under cold, running water. Wash at least 4 times or until the water runs clear. Drain.

2.Place the rice in a pot. Add the water and konbu. Cover and bring it to a boil over high heat. Remove the konbu once it starts boiling.

3.Reduce heat and let it simmer for 10 minutes. Remove from heat. Do not remove the lid. Let it sit for a few minutes to allow the rice to finish cooking.

4.Place the hot rice in a sushi-oke . If you don't have one, you may use anylarge, shallow bowl you have available. Spread the rice and pour over the awase-zu.

5. Quickly mix it together with the rice using a wooden spatula. Make quick, cutting strokes to fan the sushi rice and allow it to cool down. Do this quickly and carefully - don't break the rice grains. Let it rest until cool enough to handle. Use it immediately.

Tossa Shoyu

Tossa shoyu is a sauce made with soy sauce and dashi stock and mirin. It adds a whole depth of flavor to sashimi and sushi. You can make the sauce ahead of time and keep it in tightly-sealed container inside the fridge.

Ingredients:

- 1 tsp. dashi powder (Available in most Asian groceries.)
- 6 tbsp. water
- 6 tbsp. soy sauce
- 1 tbsp. sake or Japanese rice wine (Available in most Asian groceries.)
- 1 ½ tsp. mirin or Japanese cooking wine (Available in most Asian groceries.)

Method:

1. Place all ingredients in a small saucepan. Over low heat, bring the mixture to a boil. Reduce heat and let it simmer for a minute or two.

2.Remove from heat and let cool slightly before using.

Ponzu

Ponzu is a light and citrusy sauce which can be used as dipping sauce or dressing for salad. One of the ingredients, yuzu, is actually a type of Japanese citrus which is quite similar to lime. If you have difficulties looking for lime, ordinary lime may be substituted.

Makes 10 ounces.

Ingredients:

- 4 tbsp. cider vinegar
- 4 tbsp. rice vinegar
- 4 tbsp. lemon juice
- 4 tbsp. yuzu or lime juice
- 6 ½ tbsp. soy sauce

Method:

1. Combine all ingredients in a container with tight-fitting lid. Shake well to combine. Transfer to serving dish.

Gari

Gari or pickled ginger is a common condiment served with sushi. The slightly spicy and refreshing ginger taste pairs quite well with sushi and sashimi, too.

Makes about 2 cups.

Ingredients:

- ¾ cup fresh ginger, peeled and sliced thinly (Use a mandolin or peeler to slice.)
- 1 tsp. salt
- ¼ cup rice wine vinegar
- ¼ cup water
- ¼ cup sugar

Method:

1.Place the ginger slices in a bowl and sprinkle with salt. Mix well. Let it rest for about half an hour. Squeeze all excess liquid from the ginger. Set aside.

2. In a saucepan, simmer the rice wine vinegar, water and sugar. Cook until the sugar is dissolved. Increase the heat and let it boil. Remove from heat.

3.Place the ginger in a clean, sterilized glass container. Pour the vinegar mixture over the ginger. Let it cool for a few minutes before sealing the container. Place the ginger in the fridge overnight before using.

Nigiri

Nigiri is the typical sushi type, made with small rice balls and topped with fresh fish such as tuna, salmon or sometimes, fresh shrimp or egg roes. These are probably the easiest type of sushi that you can make and this section of the book will show you how you can make your own nigiri, too.

Salmon Nigiri

Salmon is a favorite topping for nigiri. Its rich and soft texture blends perfectly well with the light acidic taste of the sushi rice. Since this will be eaten raw, do make sure that you get the freshest salmon possible and ask if the fish you will be buying is good for sushi.

Makes about 12 pieces.

Ingredients:

- 3 cups cooked sushi rice
- salt
- 6 oz. fresh salmon fillet
- For dipping
- tossa shoyu
- wasabi paste (Available in most Asian groceries.)

Method:

1. Salt the salmon lightly and leave it in the fridge for about an hour. Slice the salmon into thin, bite-sized pieces.

2. Let the sushi rice cool down to room temperature before using. With slightly damp fingers, rub a little salt between your palms.

3. Take about two to three tablespoons of the rice and mold it into an oval shape. Flatten slightly. Repeat for the rest of the sushi rice. Add a dab of wasabi on top of each rice ball. Top each rice ball with a slice of salmon. Serve immediately together with the tossa shoyu and wasabi paste.

Tuna Nigiri

Tuna is another common topping for nigiri. Same with salmon be sure to get the freshest tuna possible. Ask for sushi-grade tuna when you buy one.

Makes about 12 pieces.

Ingredients:

- 3 cups cooked sushi rice
- salt
- 6 oz. fresh sushi-grade tuna
- For dipping
- tossa shoyu
- wasabi paste (Available in most Asian groceries.)

Method:

1. Salt the tuna lightly and leave it in the fridge for about an hour. Slice the fish into thin, bite-sized pieces.

2. Let the sushi rice cool down to room temperature before using. With slightly damp fingers, rub a little salt between your palms.

3. Take about two to three tablespoons of the rice and mold it into an oval shape. Flatten slightly. Repeat for the rest of the sushi rice. Add a dab of wasabi on top of each rice ball. Top each rice ball with a slice of tuna. Serve immediately together with the tossa shoyu and more wasabi paste.

Ebi Nigiri

Ebi or prawns is another popular nigiri topping. The prawns are lightly salted and blanched before they are placed on top of the rice.

Makes 16 pieces.

Ingredients:

- 1 cup water
- 6 tsp. salt
- 16 pcs. medium-sized prawns
- 2 cups sushi rice
- 8 pcs. shiso or perilla leaves
- For dipping
- tossa shoyu
- wasabi paste (Available in most Asian groceries.)

Method:

1. Place the water in a saucepan and bring it to a boil. Add the salt.

2. Thread each prawn along its length on a bamboo skewer.

3. Cook the prawns in the salted water for about two minutes or until they turn bright orange.

3. Quickly remove them from the hot water then immediately plunge them into a bowl of ice-cold water.

4. Drain. Remove the skewers by gently turning the prawns. Cut off the heads and remove the shells and legs.

5. Insert a knife into the underside to open them out. Remove the vein. Set aside.

6. Take the sushi rice and mold them into 16 rice balls. Flatten slightly and set aside.

7. Halve the shiso leaves. Place half a leaf on top of each prawn. Top the rice balls with the prepared prawns. Serve immediately together with tossa shoyu and wasabi paste.

Tamago Nigiri

Tamago or Japanese style omelet is an easy and delicious topping for nigiri. Almost all sushi restaurants would have this simple and humble sushi recipe and while most Japanese people buy sushi rather than make it at home, tamago nigiri is one of those they actually do make at home.

Makes about 12 pieces.

Ingredients:

- 2 cups sushi rice
- 2 sheets nori or dried seaweed (Available in most Asian groceries.)
- Tamago
- 4 eggs
- 2 tbsp. sugar
- 1 tsp. light soy sauce
- oil for pan frying

- For dipping
- tossa shoyu
- wasabi paste (Available in most Asian groceries.)

Method:

1. Prepare the tamago. Crack the eggs into a bowl. Whisk until the eggs are smooth. While whisking, stir in the sugar and soy sauce. Continue whisking lightly until everything is mixed in well.

2. Pour just enough oil to cover a medium-sized fry pan and heat it over medium-high. When the pan is hot enough, pour half of the egg mixture into the pan. When the egg starts to turn opaque, lift half of the egg with a spatula, rolling it over to the other side of the pan. Pour in half of the remaining mixture. Repeat, this time rolling the egg over to the opposite site. Do this until you run out of eggs.

3. Remove the eggs from heat and transfer it to a plate. Let cool for a while.

4. When the eggs are cool enough to handle, slice the eggs into about 2 inch strips. Set aside.

5. Cut the nori into strips, about a centimeter thick. Set aside.

6. Prepare the rice balls. Wet your hands and rub a little salt on them to prevent the rice from sticking. Mold the rice into 12 oval shaped balls.

7. Place a piece of tamago on top of each rice ball. Take a nori strip and wrap it around each nigiri. Wrap tightly, ensuring that your nigiri won't fall apart. Trim the nori

strips if they are too long. Serve immediately with tossa shoyu and wasabi paste.

Norimaki

Norimaki or rolled sushi consists of sushi rice and topping wrapped in nori sheets. These are one of the more common types of sushi, along with nigiri. Inside out norimaki is also quite popular, though more so outside of Japan. They're actually a bit rare in traditional Japanese sushi restaurants. This section of the book will show you how to make your own tasty norimaki.

Shichimi Norimaki

Shichimi torigashi is a seven-spice mix often used in both Japanese and Chinese cooking. Here, the spice is used to give an otherwise plain salmon norimaki a spicy kick.

Makes 24 pieces.

Ingredients:

- 6 oz. salmon fillet
- 3 tbsp. shichimi togarashi or seven-spice powder (Available in most Asian groceries.)
- chili flakes
- 2 cups sushi rice
- 3 sheets nori or dried seaweed (Available in most Asian groceries.)
- 2 tbsp. Japanese mayonnaise

For dipping

- tossa shoyu
- wasabi paste (Available in most Asian groceries.)

Method:

1.Dust the salmon fillet generously with the shichimi togarishi. Sprinkle over some chili flakes as well.

2. Heat the oil in a skillet over medium-high heat. Cook the salmon, about 8 minutes on both sides. Remove from heat and let it cool before flaking the fish into large pieces.

3. Divide the rice into 3 equal portions. Put a sheet of nori shiny-side down on a rolling mat with the longest end towards you.

4. Wet hands slightly. Using your hands, spread a portion of the rice in an even layer on the nori. Leave about a quarter of an inch of nori visible at the farthest end away from you.

5. Spread the mayonnaise on the rice at the end nearest you. Lay a third of the flaked salmon on top of the mayonnaise.

6. To roll the sushi, fold the mat over, starting at the end where the ingredients are. Tuck in the end of the nori when you start rolling; keep rolling lifting up the mat as you. Keep the pressure even but gentle until you finish the roll. Moisten the top edge of the nori with water to seal the sushi roll. Repeat for the remaining nori and fillings.

7. Slice each roll into about 8 even pieces, using a wet and sharp knife. Transfer to serving dish and serve together with tossa shoyu and wasabi paste.

Salmon and Asparagus Norimaki

This norimaki recipe tastes slightly sweet due to the addition of Japanese mayonnaise. Unlike US brands, Japanese mayonnaise tastes much milder and sweeter since they only use whole eggs. The combination of salmon, asparagus and mayonnaise creates a really harmonious balance of tastes. Try it!

Makes 24 pieces.

Ingredients:

- 6 pcs. asparagus spears
- 1 cup water
- 6 oz. salmon fillet
- 1 tbsp. oil
- 2 cups sushi rice
- 6 small sheets nori or dried seaweed (Available in most Asian groceries.)
- wasabi paste (Available in most Asian groceries.)

- 1 tbsp. Japanese mayonnaise
- 1 tsp. toasted sesame seeds

For dipping

- tossa shoyu

Method:

1. Place the water in a skillet. Lay the asparagus spears flat in the skillet and let it simmer over medium-high heat. Cook until the asparagus is tender. Slice each spear into 3 inch pieces. Set aside.

2. Heat the oil in a skillet over medium-high heat. Cook the salmon for about 8 minutes on both sides. Remove from heat and let cool. Flake the salmon into large pieces. Set aside.

3. Divide the rice into 6 equal portions. Put a sheet of nori shiny-side down on a rolling mat with the longest end towards you.

4. Wet hands slightly. Using your hands, spread a portion of the rice in an even layer on the nori. Leave about a quarter of an inch of nori visible at the farthest end away from you.

5. Dab some wasabi on top of the rice. Spread the mayonnaise on the rice at the end nearest you. Lay a third of the flaked salmon on top of the mayonnaise. Lay an asparagus spear on top of the mayonnaise and put some of the salmon next to it.

6. To roll the sushi, fold the mat over, starting at the end where the ingredients are. Tuck in the end of the nori when you start rolling; keep rolling lifting up the mat as you. Keep the pressure even but gentle until you finish the roll. Moisten the top edge of the nori with water to seal the sushi roll. Repeat for the remaining nori and fillings.

7. Slice each roll into smaller pieces, using a wet and sharp knife. Transfer to serving dish and serve together with tossa shoyu.

Shrimp and Avocado Norimaki

While avocado is not traditionally used as a filling for norimaki, it's quite popular nowadays. In this recipe, avocado is paired with shrimp giving this filling a rich and creamy texture.

Makes 6 rolls.

Ingredients:

- 2 cups sushi rice
- 6 small sheets nori or dried seaweed (Available in most Asian groceries.)
- 1 tbsp. Japanese mayonnaise
- 1 tsp. lemon zest
- 12 pcs. jumbo shrimp, cooked, shelled and deveined
- 2 ripe avocado, cut into strips
- 1 small cucumber, peeled and cut into strips

For dipping

- tossa shoyu
- wasabi paste (Available in most Asian groceries.)

Method:

1. Divide the rice into 6 equal portions. Put a sheet of nori shiny-side down on a rolling mat with the longest end towards you.

2. Wet hands slightly. Using your hands, spread a portion of the rice in an even layer on the nori. Leave about a quarter of an inch of nori visible at the farthest end away from you.

3. Mix the mayonnaise with the lemon zest. Spread some onto the rice at the end nearest you. Place 2 shrimps on top of the mayonnaise then layer a few avocado strips on top. Lay a line of cucumber strips beside the avocado.

4. To roll the sushi, fold the mat over, starting at the end where the ingredients are. Tuck in the end of the nori when you start rolling; keep rolling lifting up the mat as you. Keep the pressure even but gentle until you finish the roll. Moisten the top edge of the nori with water to seal the sushi roll. Repeat for the remaining nori and fillings.

5. Slice each roll into about 8 even pieces, using a wet and sharp knife. Transfer to serving dish and serve together with tossa shoyu and wasabi paste.

Crab Asparagus and Shiitake Norimaki with Ponzu Sauce

This norimaki recipe makes use of ponzu sauce instead of the more traditional tossa shoyu for dipping. It pairs really well with the crab, asparugus and shiitake mushroom filling. Try it!

Makes 24 pieces.

Ingredients:

- 6 pcs. asparagus spears
- 1 cup water
- 1 tbsp. oil
- 2 cups sushi rice
- 6 small sheets nori or dried seaweed (Available in most Asian groceries.)
- wasabi paste (Available in most Asian groceries.)
- 6 crab sticks
- ¼ cup ponzu sauce

Method:

1. Place the water in a skillet and bring it to a boil over medium-high heat. Lay the asparagus spears flat and let it simmer until tender. Remove from heat and slice into 3 inch pieces. Set aside.

2. Heat the oil in a small pan. Stir-fry the mushrooms for about 5 minutes or until they are completely soft.

3.Divide the rice into 6 equal portions. Put a sheet of nori shiny-side down on a rolling mat with the longest end towards you.

4. Wet hands slightly. Using your hands, spread a portion of the rice in an even layer on the nori. Leave about a quarter of an inch of nori visible at the farthest end away from you.

5.Dab some wasabi on top of the rice. Lay an asparagus spear on top, then add two crabsticks next to it. Add a line of mushrooms.

6. To roll the sushi, fold the mat over, starting at the end where the ingredients are. Tuck in the end of the nori when you start rolling; keep rolling lifting up the mat as you. Keep the pressure even but gentle until you finish the roll. Moisten the top edge of the nori with water to seal the sushi roll. Repeat for the remaining nori and fillings.

7. Slice each roll into even pieces, using a wet and sharp knife. Transfer to serving dish and serve together with tossa shoyu and wasabi paste.

Dragon Roll

Unagi or eel and crab meat create a really delicious filling for this aptly named inside-out norimaki, dragon roll. Prepared unagi marinated with a sweet soy-based sauce is readily available in most Japanese groceries.

Makes about 8 pcs.

Ingredients:

- 2 large sheets nori or dried seaweed (Available in most Asian groceries)
- 1 cup sushi rice
- 8 tbsp. cooked crabmeat
- 3 oz. mizuna or baby greens, similar to arugula (Available in most Asian groceries.)
- 2 pcs. prepared unagi fillet, trimmed to fit the nori sheet (Available in most Asian groceries.)

Ginger wasabi mayonnaise

- 4 tbsp. Japanese mayonnaise
- 2 tsp. wasabi paste(Available in most Asian groceries.)
- 1 tsp. ginger, peeled and grated

Dipping

- tossa shoyu
- wasabi paste(Available in most Asian groceries.)

Method:

1.Prepare the ginger wasabi mayonnaise. In a small bowl, combine the mayonnaise, wasabi and ginger. Mix well and set aside.

2. Divide the rice into 2 equal parts. Line a rolling mat with plastic wrap to prevent the rice from sticking. Put a sheet of nori, shiny-side down on a rolling mat with the longest end towards you.

3. Wet hands slightly. Using your hands, spread a portion of the rice in an even layer on the nori. Leave about a quarter of an inch of nori visible at the farthest end away from you. Lay another sheet of plastic on top. Turn it over. Carefully remove the plastic from the nori.

4.Place the crabmeat in the middle of the nori. Lay the avocado strips on either side of the crabmeat. Top with the mizuna. Drizzle the ginger wasabi mayonnaise on top.

5. To roll the sushi, fold the mat over, starting at the end where the ingredients are. Tuck in the end of the nori when you start rolling; keep rolling lifting up the mat as you. Keep the pressure even but gentle until you finish the roll.

6. Carefully wrap the unagi around each roll. Secure with a toothpick if needed.

7. Slice each roll into 4 even pieces, using a wet and sharp knife. Transfer to serving dish and serve together with tossa shoyu and wasabi .

California Roll

Crab sticks are the star of this norimaki recipe! They are a favorite filling in norimaki recipes because of their neat shape.

Makes 24 pieces.

Ingredients:

- 2 cups sushi rice
- 6 small sheets nori or dried seaweed (Available in most Asian groceries.)
- wasabi paste (Available in most Asian groceries.)
- ½ ripe avocado, cut into strips
- 6 pcs. crab sticks, split in half lengthwise
- 1 small cucumber, peeled and cut into strips

For dipping

- light soy sauce

Method:

1. Divide the rice into 6 equal portions. Put a sheet of nori, shiny-side down on a rolling mat with the longest end towards you.

2. Wet hands slightly. Using your hands, spread a portion of the rice in an even layer on the nori. Leave about a quarter of an inch of nori visible at the farthest end away from you.

3.Dab some wasabi on top of the rice. Place 2 avocado slices on top. Add 2 slices of crabsticks and finish off with a line of cucumber slices.

4. To roll the sushi, fold the mat over, starting at the end where the ingredients are. Tuck in the end of the nori when you start rolling; keep rolling lifting up the mat as you. Keep the pressure even but gentle until you finish the roll. Moisten the top edge of the nori with water to seal the sushi roll. Repeat for the remaining nori and fillings.

5. Slice each roll into 4 even pieces, using a wet and sharp knife. Transfer to serving dish and serve together with soy sauce and wasabi paste.

Inside-out California Norimaki

Give your California a twist by turning it inside out! The outside is covered with toasted sesame seeds giving it nice, slightly nutty flavor.

Makes 24 pieces.

Ingredients:

- 2 cups sushi rice
- 6 small sheets nori or dried seaweed, cut into 4 strips lengthwise (Available in most Asian groceries.)
- ¼ ripe avocado, cut into strips
- 6 pcs. crabsticks, halved
- 1 small cucumber, peeled and julienned
- 3 tbsp. toasted sesame seeds

Method:

1. Divide the rice into 6 equal parts. Line a rolling mat with plastic wrap to prevent the rice from sticking. Put a sheet of nori, shiny-side down on a rolling mat with the longest end towards you.

2. Wet hands slightly. Using your hands, spread a portion of the rice in an even layer on the nori. Leave about a quarter of an inch of nori visible at the farthest end away from you. Lay another sheet of plastic on top. Turn it over. Carefully remove the plastic from the nori.

3. Place some avocado in the middle of the nori. Keep it parallel to the edge nearest you. Add 2 slices of crabsticks and finish off with a line of cucumber slices.

4. To roll the sushi, fold the mat over, starting at the end where the ingredients are. Tuck in the end of the nori when you start rolling; keep rolling lifting up the mat as you. Keep the pressure even but gentle until you finish the roll.

5. Place the sesame seeds on a large plate. Roll the finished norimaki to coat them. Repeat for the remaining nori and fillings.

6. Slice each roll into 4 even pieces, using a wet and sharp knife. Transfer to serving dish and serve together with soy sauce and wasabi paste.

Inside-out Salmon Norimaki

The outside of this norimaki recipe is covered with tobiko or flying-fish roe, adding a delicate and salty taste. Serve it together with tossa shoyu and wasabi.

Makes about 8 pieces.

Ingredients

- 1 cup sushi rice
- 2 large nori sheets or dried seaweed (Available in most Asian groceries.)
- 4 oz. fresh salmon fillet, cut into strips
- 1 small avocado, cut into strips
- 3 tbsp. tobiko or flying-fish roe

Ginger wasabi mayonnaise

- 4 tbsp. Japanese mayonnaise
- 2 tsp. wasabi paste(Available in most Asian groceries.)
- 1 tsp. ginger, peeled and grated

Dipping

- tossa shoyu
- wasabi paste(Available in most Asian groceries.)

Method:

1. Prepare the ginger wasabi mayonnaise. In a small bowl, combine the mayonnaise, wasabi and ginger. Mix well and set aside.

2. Divide the rice into 2 equal parts. Line a rolling mat with plastic wrap to prevent the rice from sticking. Put a sheet of nori, shiny-side down on a rolling mat with the longest end towards you.

3. Wet hands slightly. Using your hands, spread a portion of the rice in an even layer on the nori. Leave about a quarter of an inch of nori visible at the farthest end away from you. Lay another sheet of plastic on top. Turn it over. Carefully remove the plastic from the nori.

4. Place the salmon strips in the middle of the nori. Lay the avocado strips on either side of the salmon. Drizzle the ginger wasabi mayonnaise on top.

5. To roll the sushi, fold the mat over, starting at the end where the ingredients are. Tuck in the end of the nori when you start rolling; keep rolling lifting up the mat as you. Keep the pressure even but gentle until you finish the roll.

6. Place the tobiko on a large plate. Roll the finished norimaki to coat them. Repeat for the remaining nori and fillings.

7. Slice each roll into 4 even pieces, using a wet and sharp knife. Transfer to serving dish and serve together with tossa shoyu and wasabi .

Gunkan

Gunkan sushi look like tiny boats made of sushi rice and nori. They are then topped with various fillings, the most common being fish eggs and sea urchin. This section of the book will show you how to make your own delicious gunkanzushi.

Tobiko Gunkanzushi

Tobiko or flying-fish roe is one of the most common toppings for this type of sushi. The roe can be quite slippery that's why the boat-shaped gunkan can hold in fillings like thisbquite well. Serve it with tossa shoyu, wasabi and a little gari on the side.

Makes about 8 pieces

Ingredients:

- 1 cup sushi rice
- 2 sheets nori or dried seaweed, cut into four strips
- 1 tbsp. wasabi paste (Available in most Asian groceries.)
- 4 oz. tobiko or flying fish roe

Dipping

- tossa shoyu
- wasabi paste(Available in most Asian groceries.)
- gari or pickled ginger

Method:

1. Divide the rice into 8 portions.

2. Wet hands slightly. Shape each portion of rice into a small oval.

3.Take a strip of nori and carefully wrap it around the rice. Trim off any excess and join the ends together with some crushed grains of rice.

4. Dab a little wasabi on top of the rice. Top with about a spoonful of the tobiko. Repeat for the rest of the rice ovals. Serve together tossa shoyu, wasabi and a little gari on the side.

Salmon Roe Gunkanzushi

Salmon roe is one of the most popular fillings for gunkan. Not only does it taste delicious, it also looks very pretty with its bright, orange hue.

Makes 16 pieces.

Ingredients:

- 2 cups sushi rice
- 4 small sheets nori or dried seaweed, cut into 4 strips lengthwise (Available in most Asian groceries.)wasabi
- 3/4 cup salmon roe

Dipping

- soy sauce

Method:

1. Divide the rice into 16 portions.

2. Wet hands slightly. Shape each portion of rice into a small oval.

3.Take a strip of nori and carefully wrap it around the rice. Trim off any excess and join the ends together with some crushed grains of rice.

4. Dab a little wasabi on top of the rice. Top with about a spoonful of the salmon roe. Repeat for the rest of the rice ovals. Serve together with soy sauce and some wasabi paste.

Negitoro Gunkanzushi

Tuna has always been a traditional sushi topping and of course, gunkanzushi would have its version, too!

Makes about 8 pieces

Ingredients:

- 4 oz. tuna, chopped
- 4 stalks green onions
- 1 tbsp. soy sauce
- 1 tsp. shichimi togarashi or or seven-spice powder (Available in most Asian groceries.)
- 1 cup sushi rice
- 2 sheets nori or dried seaweed, cut into four strips
- 1 tbsp. wasabi paste Available in most Asian groceries.)

Dipping

- tossa shoyu
- wasabi paste(Available in most Asian groceries.)

Method:

1. In a bowl, mix together the tuna, green onions, soy sauce and shichimi. Set aside.

2.Divide the rice into 8 portions.

3. Wet hands slightly. Shape each portion of rice into a small oval.

4.Take a strip of nori and carefully wrap it around the rice. Trim off any excess and join the ends together with some crushed grains of rice.

5. Dab a little wasabi on top of the rice. Top with about a spoonful of the prepared tuna filling. Repeat for the rest of the rice ovals. Serve together tossa shoyu and wasabi.

Crayfish and Mango Gunkanzushi

Crayfish tastes quite similar to crab but with the texture of lobster. Its mild taste pairs really well with the tartness of mangoes. Try it!

Makes about 8 pieces.

Ingredients:

- 4 oz. crayfish, cooked, shelled and chopped
- 1 large mango, peeled and cho[[ed
- 1 tbsp. lime juice
- 1 cup sushi rice
- 2 sheets nori or dried seaweed, cut into four strips
- 1 tbsp. wasabi paste (Available in most Asian groceries.)

Dipping

- tossa shoyu
- wasabi paste (Available in most Asian groceries.)

Method:

1. In a bowl, mix together the crayfish, mango and lime juice. Set aside.

2. Divide the rice into 8 portions.

3. Wet hands slightly. Shape each portion of rice into a small oval.

4. Take a strip of nori and carefully wrap it around the rice. Trim off any excess and join the ends together with some crushed grains of rice.

5. Dab a little wasabi on top of the rice. Top with about a spoonful of the prepared crayfish filling.Repeat for the rest of the rice ovals. Serve together tossa shoyu and wasabi.

Lemon Pepper Crab Gunkanzushi

Give your crab topping an elegant and delicate touch!
Lightly flavored with lemon and pepper, this sushi recipe is
definitely going to delight your taste buds.

Makes about 16 pieces.

Ingredients:

- ½ cup cooked crabmeat
- 2 tsp. grated lemon zest
- 2 tsp. pepper
- 4 tbsp. Japanese mayonnaise
- salt
- 1 ½ cups sushi rice
- 4 small sheets nori or dried seaweed, cut into 4
  strips lengthwise
- juice from 1 lemon

Garnish

- 1 lemon, quartered
- wasabi paste (Available from most Asian
  groceries.)
- gari or pickled ginger

Method:

1. In a bowl, mix together the lemon, pepper, mayonnaise and crabmeat. Season it with salt. Set aside.

2.Divide the rice into 16 portions.

3. Wet hands slightly. Shape each portion of rice into a small oval.

4.Take a strip of nori and carefully wrap it around the rice. Trim off any excess and join the ends together with some crushed grains of rice.

5.Spoon a little of the crab mixture on top of the rice. Squeeze a little lemon juice on top. Repeat for the remaining rice balls. Serve immediately together with the gari, wasabi and lemon wedges.

Greenbeans Gunkanzushi with Gomadare Sauce

Gomadare sauce is a sesame-based sweet sauce, often used for shabu-shabu. Here this uniquely Japanese sauce is paired with an all-veggie gunkanzushi. Try it!

Makes about 8 pieces.

Ingredients:

- 4 oz. green beans, blanched and sliced
- 2 sheets nori or dried seaweed, cut into 4 strips (Available in most Asian groceries.)

Gomadare sauce

- 4 tbsp. toasted sesame seeds
- 1/2 tsp. sugar
- 1 tbsp. dark miso paste (Available in most Asian groceries.)
- 1 tbsp. mirin or Japanese cooking wine (Available in most Asian groceries.)

Method:

1. Prepare the gomadare sauce. Grind the sesame seeds using a mortar and pestle.

2. Add the sugar, miso and mirin. Mix well. Add the sauce to the blanched green beans. Make sure to coat the beans well.

3. Divide the rice into 8 portions. Wet hands slightly. Shape

each portion of rice into a small oval.

4. Take a strip of nori and carefully wrap it around the rice. Trim off any excess and join the ends together with some crushed grains of rice.

5. Top with about a spoonful of the prepared green beans filling. Repeat for the rest of the rice ovals. Serve together with the gomadare sauce.

Temaki

Temaki literally translates to hand-rolls. It's definitely quite unique-looking, resembling ice cream cones filled with various toppings. They can actually be much easier to create rather than the more traditional nigiri and norimaki. However, unlike the former two, temaki is quite larger in size and can be quite difficult to pick up and eat. This section of the book will be showing you how to create this delicious and unique-looking sushi.

Unagi Temaki

Smoked unagi or eel is a favorite dish among local Japanese. Glazed with some sweet mirin sauce - the taste is definitely out of this world! Serve it with some gari or pickled ginger on the side.

Makes about 12 pieces.

Ingredients:

- 1 cup soy sauce
- 4 tbsp. mirin or Japanese cooking wine (Available in most Asian groceries.)
- 4 tbsp. sake or Japanese rice wine (Available in most Asian groceries.)

- 3 tbsp. honey
- 6 large sheets nori or dried seaweed (Available in most Asian groceries.)
- 1 cup sushi rice
- 4 smoked eel, cut into strips
- 1 ripe avocado, cut into strips
- gari or pickled ginger

Method:

1. Prepare the glaze. In a saucepan, combine together the soy sauce, mirin and sake. Simmer over medium-high heat for about 5 minutes. Stir in the honey. Remove from heat and set aside.

2. Prepare the temaki. Halve the nori sheets. Take one half and lay it on a flat surface. Spread some rice on top, about 2/3 of the sheet. Place some unagi top of the rice. Brush the eel with the prepared glaze. Lay a couple of avocado slices beside the unagi.

3. Roll the temaki into a cone, folding the bottom corner in as you roll. Use some crushed rice grains to keep the temaki in place. Repeat with the remaining ingredients. Transfer to serving dish and serve with pickled ginger on the side.

Tuna Temaki

If you're one of those who do not like raw tuna in their sushi, then this recipe is for you. Enjoy the goodness of fresh tuna in this temaki recipe. Serve it with either ponzu sauce or tossa shoyu and wasabi.

Makesabout 12 pieces.

Ingredients:

- 12 oz. fresh tuna fillet
- 2 tsp. pepper
- 2 tsp. sesame seeds
- 2 tbsp. ginger, peeled and grated
- salt
- 4 tbsp. vegetable oil
- 6 large sheets nori or toasted seaweed (Available in most Asian groceries.)
- 1 cup sushi rice

- 1 cucumber, peeled and cut into strips
- 8 tbsp. Japanese mayonnaise
- wasabi paste (Available in most Asian groceries.)

Dipping

- tossa shoyu or ponzu sauce

Method:

1. In a small bowl, mix together the pepper, ginger and sesame seeds. Take your tuna and rub this mixture all over the fish. Season it lightly with salt. Set aside.

2. Heat the oil in a small pan. Sear the tuna for about 6 minutes. Remove from heat and let it cool. When it is cool enough to handle, slice the tuna into thin slices.

3. Prepare the temaki. Halve the nori sheets. Take one half and lay it on a flat surface. Spread some rice on top, about 2/3 of the sheet. Place some tuna slices and cucumber on top of the rice. Top with some mayonnaise and wasabi.

4. Roll the temaki into a cone, folding the bottom corner in as you roll. Use some crushed rice grains to keep the temaki in place. Repeat with the remaining ingredients. Transfer to serving dish and serve with tossa shoyu or ponzu sauce for dipping.

Squid Temaki

Sichuan pepper is used to flavor the squid for this temaki recipe, giving it that nice, zesty taste. You may want to skip out on dipping it in wasabi since this recipe can get quite spicy.

Makes about 6 pieces.

Ingredients:

- 12 pcs. squid rings
- 4 tbsp. all-purpose flour
- 1 tsp. Sichuan pepper (Available in most Asian groceries.)
- 1 tsp. sea salt
- oil, for frying
- 3 large sheets nori or dried seaweed, halved (Available in most Asian groceries.)
- 1 cup sushi rice
- 4 tbsp. Japanese mayonnaise

Method:

1. Cut the squid rings in half. Set aside.

2. Mix the flour and Sichuan pepper together with the salt. Rub this mixture all over the squid. Make sure to coat it well.

3. In a wok, heat enough oil to fry the squid. Fry the squid in batches. Drain off excess oil with paper towels.

4. Prepare the temaki. Halve the nori sheets. Take one half

and lay it on a flat surface. Spread some rice on top, about 2/3 of the sheet. Place some squid rings top of the rice. Top with some mayonnaise.

5. Roll the temaki into a cone, folding the bottom corner in as you roll. Use some crushed rice grains to keep the temaki in place. Repeat with the remaining ingredients. Transfer to serving dish and serve immediately.

Salmon Temaki with Sweet Chili Sauce

Give your temaki with a strikingly delicious kick - sweet chili sauce for dipping! While tossa shoyu is the traditional dip for sushi, sweet chili actually pairs very well with salmon. Makes about 12 pieces.

Ingredients:

- 12 os. salmon fillet
- salt
- pepper
- 2 tbsp. vegetable oil
- 6 large sheets nori or dried seaweed (Available in most Asian groceries.)
- 1 cup sushi rice
- 4 stalks green onions, sliced
- 8 tbsp. Japanese mayonnaise
- sweet chili sauce

Method:

1. Season the salmon with salt and pepper. Set aside.

2. Heat the oil in a skillet over medium-high heat. Cook the salmon, skin-side down first. Let it brown for about 2 minutes before flipping to the other side. Let it cook for another 2 minutes. Remove from heat. Let cool before flaking into pieces. Set aside.

3. Halve the nori sheets. Take one half and lay it on a flat surface. Spread some rice on top, about 2/3 of the sheet. Put some salmon and green onions on top of the rice. Drizzle with some mayonnaise and sweet chili sauce.

4. Roll the temaki into a cone, folding the bottom corner in as you roll. Use some crushed rice grains to keep the temaki in place. Repeat with the remaining ingredients. Transfer to serving dish and serve with some sweet chili sauce.

Crispy Salmon Skin Temaki

Salmon skin tastes wonderful, especially when it's grilled to a crisp. It provides a delicious contrast to the soft, fluffy seasoned sushi rice.

Makes about 4.

Ingredients:

- 1 cup sushi rice
- 2 large sheets nori or dried seaweed, halved (Available in most Asian groceries)
- 1 tsp. salt
- 2 postcard-sized salmon skin
- 1 tsp. wasabi paste (Available in most Asian groceries)
- 1 spring onion, chopped
- 3 oz. mizuna or baby greens, similar to arugula (Available in most Asian groceries.)

Method:

1. Sprinkle the salt all over the salmon skin. Grill the skin until it becomes crisp. Let cool for a minute then slice the skin into thin strips.

2. In a bowl, combine the salmon skin, wasabi paste, spring onion and mizuna.

3.Halve the nori sheets. Take one half and lay it on a flat surface. Spread some rice on top, about 2/3 of the sheet. Place ¼ of the prepare salmion skin filling on top of the rice. D

4. Roll the temaki into a cone, folding the bottom corner in as you roll. Use some crushed rice grains to keep the temaki in place. Repeat with the remaining ingredients. Transfer to serving dish and serve with some tossa shoyu and wasabi.

Codfish Temaki with Tartar Sauce

This is another unique filling idea for temaki - codfish cooked in goujon style with delectably creamytartar sauce! This is definitely a perfect blend of eastern and western cooking. Give it a try.

Makes about 12 pieces.

Ingredients:

- 12 oz. codfish fillet, cut into strips
- salt
- pepper
- ½ cup panko or Japanese bread crumbs
- vegetable oil for deep frying
- 6 large sheets nori or seaweed (Available in most Asian groceries.)
- 1 cup sushi rice
- Sauce
- ½ cup mayonnaise
- 1 tsp. sweet pickle relish
- ½ tsp. yellow mustard
- ½ tsp. lemon juice

Dipping

- wasabi paste (Available in most Asian groceries.)

Method:

1. Prepare the tartar sauce. In a mixing bowl combine all sauce ingredients - mayonnaise, pickle relish, mustard and lemon juice. Mix well. Chill in the fridge until ready to use.

2. Season the fish with salt and pepper. Coat with panko. Set aside.

3. Heat the oil in a deep fryer over medium-high heat. Deep fry the fish until it turns golden brown. Place the cooked fish on paper towels to drain excess oil.

4. Prepare the temaki. Halve the nori sheets. Take one half and lay it on a flat surface. Spread some rice on top, about 2/3 of the sheet. Place some fried cod on top of the rice. Drizzle with some prepared tartar sauce.

5. Roll the temaki into a cone, folding the bottom corner in as you roll. Use some crushed rice grains to keep the temaki in place. Repeat with the remaining ingredients. Transfer to serving dish and serve with wasabi and the remaining tartar sauce.

Vegetarian Temaki

Here's a meat and seafood-free version of temaki. The fillings used are cucumber, carrots and asparagus, but you can actually add other vegetables as you wish. Thinly sliced daikon would also taste great as a filling for this recipe. Serve it with some gari and tossa shoyu.

Makes about 6 pieces.

Ingredients:

- 1 cup sushi rice
- 3 large sheets nori or dried seaweed (Available in most Asian groceries.)
- 1 small cucumber, peeled and julienned
- 1 small carrot, peeled and julienned
- 6 pcs. asparagus spears, blanched
- 3 tsp. white sesame, toasted

Dipping

- gari or pickled ginger
- tossa shoyu

Method:

1. Prepare the temaki. Halve the nori sheets. Take one half and lay it on a flat surface. Spread some rice on top, about 2/3 of the sheet. Arrange the cucumber, carrots and asparagus spears on top. Sprinkle some toasted sesame seeds on top.

2. Roll the temaki into a cone, folding the bottom corner in as you roll. Use some crushed rice grains to keep the temaki in place. Repeat with the remaining ingredients. Transfer to serving dish and serve immediately with gari and tossa shoyu.

Chirashizushi

Some people call chirashizushi an open-faced sushi. The fillings are spread on top of the seasoned sushi rice instead of being rolled or shaped into balls. This section of the book will show you how to make yummy chirashizushi dishes.

Tokyo-style Chirashizushi

The Tokyo-style chirashizushi is a very colorful and tasty dish, made with a variety of sashimi or raw sushi toppings. Serve it with some soy sauce and gari on the side.

Makes 4 servings.

Ingredients:

- 2 cups sushi rice
- 4 tbsp. daikon or Japanese radish, peeled and shredded
- 4 tsp. cress
- 5 oz. fresh tuna steak, cut into 8 thin slices
- 5 oz. mackerel, cut into 8 thin slices
- 5 oz. salmon fillet, cut into 8 thin slices
- 4 pcs. tiger prawns, blanched, peeled and deveined
- 4 tsp. salmon roe
- 1 small cucumber, peeled and sliced

- 4 tsp. wasabi paste (Available in most Asian groceries.)

Dipping

- gari or pickled ginger
- soy sauce

Method:

1. Divide the rice evenly between 4 serving bowl. The idea is to cover the entire surface with a colorful arrangement of sashimi pieces.

2. Place a teaspoon of daikon on one side. Add some cress beside it. Carefully arrange the fish, shellfish roe and cucumber slices. Place a small dot of wasabi on one corner. Serve immediately with gari and soy sauce.

Shrimp and Crab Chirashizushi

Have a seafood feast with this recipe! Shrimp and crab are the stars of this chirashizushi recipe which are lightly flavored with lemon for a refreshing, citrusy taste.

Makes 4 servings.

Ingredients:

- 6 large raw shrimp, shelled and deveined
- 1 tbsp. oil
- ½ cup cooked crabmeat
- 2 cups sushi rice
- juice and zest from 1 lemon
- 1 ripe avocado, cut into strips1 small cucumber, peeled and cut into strips

Method:

1. Heat the oil in small pan. Quickly cook the shrimp for a few minutes, until they turn pink.Set aside.

2. In a bowl, mix together the sushi rice with the lemon juice and sest.

3. Divide the rice between 4 serving bowls. Arrange the shrimp, crab, avocado and cucumber strips on top. Serve.

Lobster Chirashizushi with Wasabi Mayonnaise

Fresh lobster on top of deliciously seasoned rice - yum! And to make it even better, wasabi flavored mayonnaise is generously drizzled on top of the lobster.

Makes 4 servings.

Ingredients:

- 1 lobster, cooked, meat removed from the shell
- 2 tbsp. Japanese mayonnaise
- 1 tsp. wasabi paste (Available in most Asian groceries.)
- 2 cups sushi rice
- 1 tbsp. gari or pickled ginger chopped
- 1 small cucumber, peeled and sliced

1. Slice the lobster meat into big chunks. Set aside.

2. In a small bowl, mix the mayonnaise and wasabi together.

3. In another bowl, mix the rice with the chopped gari. Divide the rice between 4 serving bowls. Arrange the lobster, cucumber and avocado on top of the rice. Generously drizzle with wasabi mayonnaise. Serve immediately.

Smoked Mackerel Chirashizushi

Smoked mackerel is paired here with fresh daikon, giving this dish a nice, crisp texture.

Makes 4 servings.

Ingredients:

- 8 pcs. snow peas
- 1 cup water
- 1 tsp. salt
- 2 inch piece daikon or Japanese radish, peeled and shredded
- 2 cups sushi rice
- juice and zest of 1 lemon
- 2 stalks green onions, chopped
- 2 pcs. smoked mackerel, skinned and sliced into strips
- 1 small cucumber, peeled and cut into strips
- gari or pickled ginger
- wasabi paste (Available in most Asian groceries.)

Method:

1.Boil the water in a small saucepan. Add the salt and snowpeas. Cook for about 1 minute. Drain. Set aside.

2.Mix the sushi rice with the lemon juice and zest. Divide the rice between 4 serving bowls.

3.Arrange the smoked mackerel, snow peas, daikon, cucumber and green onions on top of the rice. Serve immediately together with the gari and wasabi.

Oshizushi

Oshizushi is pressed into a wooden box, before they are sliced into pieces. The box used for making oshizushi is called an oshi-waku. This is quite convenient when making sushi for bento boxes. This section of the book will show you how to make your own delicious oshizushi that you can easily pack for lunch.

Smoked Salmon with Avocado Oshizushi

Smoked salmon is an ideal topping for oshizushi as it keeps quite well. Not only that, it's also flavorful, too!

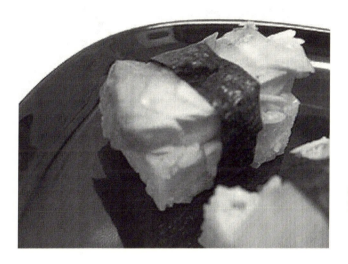

Makes about 10 pieces.

Ingredients:

- 1 cup sushi rice
- 2 tbsp. Japanese mayonnaise
- 2 tsp. lemon zest
- 6 oz. smoked salmon
- 1 large ripe avocado, cut into strips
- gari or pickled ginger
- wasabi paste (Available in most Asian groceries.)

Method:

1. Grease your oshi-waku with a little oil. If you don't have one, you can substitute a terrine mold.

2. Pack the greased oshi-waku with rice, about 1/3 full.

3. In a small bowl, mix together the mayonnaise and lemon sest. Spread this mixture evenly on top of the rice.

4. Layer the rice with smoked salmon and avocado strips. Cover the top with plastic wrap. Cover and weigh it down with something heavy (canned goods work great). Chill in the fridge for about 15 minutes.

5. Remove the sushi from the mold, pushing it out carefully. Slice into bars using a wet, sharp knife. Serve with gari and wasabi.

Teriyaki Tuna Oshizushi

Teriyaki sauce is mildly sweet and savory sauce often used for meat such as pork and chicken. Here, teriyaki sauce is spread over tuna slices and sprinkled over with toasted sesame seeds. Delicious!

Makes about 10 pieces.

Ingredients:

- 7 oz. tuna fillet, sliced thinly
- 2 tbsp. teriyaki sauce
- 1 tbsp. oil
- 10 pcs. green beans, blanched
- oil, for frying
- 1 tsp. toasted sesame seeds
- 1 cup sushi rice
- 2 tbsp. Japanese mayonnaise
- gari or pickled ginger
- wasabi paste (Available in most Asian groceries.)

Method:

1. Brush the tuna slices with the teriyaki sauce.

2. Heat the oil in a small skillet. Sear the tuna slices quickly, about 1 minute on each side. Remove from heat and set aside.

3. Halve the blanched green beans. Set aside.

4. Grease your oshi-waku with a little oil. If you don't have one, you can substitute a terrine mold. Pack the greased

oshi-waku with rice, about 1/3 full.

5. Spread the mayonnaise evenly on top of the rice. Layer the rice with tuna and green beans. Cover the top with plastic wrap. Cover and weigh it down with something heavy (canned goods work great). Chill in the fridge for about 15 minutes.

6. Remove the sushi from the mold, pushing it out carefully. Slice into bars using a wet, sharp knife. Sprinkle the sesame seeds on top. Serve with gari and wasabi.

Scallop Oshizushi

Give your oshizushi an elegantly beautiful touch! Serve your scallop oshizushi on half-shells, making them the perfect appetizer for parties. It's fairly easy and you'll surely wow your guests with its deliciously refreshing taste.

Makes 4 servings.

Ingredients:

- 10 large scallops, cleaned; reserve their shells
- 1 tbsp. oil
- juice and zest of 1 lime
- 1 cup sushi rice
- ¼ cup cilantro leaves, chopped
- wasabi paste (Available in most Asian groceries.)
- mayonnaise
- gari or pickled ginger, shredded

Method:

1. Heat the oil in a skillet. Quickly sear the scallops for about a minute or so. Remove from heat. Drizzle about half of the lime juice over the scallops. Set aside.

2. Mix the sushi rice with the remaining lime juice and zest.

3. Divide the rice between the 10 half shells. Make a small, neat mound on each one. Flatten the top a little.

4. Place a scallop on top of each rice mound. Add the cilantro leaves and garnish with a dot of wasabi and mayonnaise. Top with the shredded gari. Serve immediately.

Your feedback is important to us. It would be greatly appreciated if you could please take a moment to **REVIEW** this book on Amazon so that we could make our next version better!

Made in the USA
Lexington, KY
11 January 2014